Platform
Papers

Quarterly essays from Currency House   No. 9: July 2006

CURRENCY HOUSE

PLATFORM PAPERS
Quarterly essays from Currency House Inc.
Editor: Dr John Golder, j.golder@unsw.edu.au

Currency House Inc. is a non-profit association and resource centre advocating the role of the performing arts in public life by research, debate and publication.
Postal address: PO Box 2270, Strawberry Hills, NSW 2012, Australia
Email: info@currencyhouse.org.au   Tel: (02) 9319 4953
Website: www.currencyhouse.org.au   Fax: (02) 9319 3649
Executive Officer: Polly Rowe
Editorial Board: Katharine Brisbane AM, Dr John Golder, John McCallum, Greig Tillotson

ISBN 0 97573 015 0
ISSN 1449-583X

Cover design by Kate Florance
Typeset in 10.5 Arrus BT
Printed by Hyde Park Press, Adelaide

This edition of Platform Papers is supported by donations from the following: the Keir Foundation, Katharine Brisbane, Malcolm Duncan, David Marr, Tony Scotford, Alan Seymour, Greg and Fiona Quirk, Mary Vallentine and Jane Westbrook. To them and to all our supporters Currency House extends sincere gratitude.

Contents

AVAILABILITY *Platform Papers*, quarterly essays on the performing arts, is published every January, April, July and October and is available through bookshops or by subscription. For order form, see page 56.

LETTERS Currency House invites readers to submit letters of 400–1,000 words in response to the essays. Letters should be emailed to the Editor at info@currencyhouse.org.au or posted to Currency House at PO Box 2270, Strawberry Hills, NSW 2012, Australia. To be considered for the next issue, the letters must be received by 7 August 2006.

CURRENCY HOUSE For membership details, see our website at: www.currencyhouse.org.au

What price a creative economy?

STUART CUNNINGHAM

Author's acknowledgements

A lot of the research laid out here is a result of the ideas incubator that was Creative Industries Research and Applications Centre at Queensland University of Technology, which I was privileged to direct during its lifespan, 2001–05. My thanks go to the Australian Research Council that funded some of the research whose results are outlined here, and awarded the ARC Centre of Excellence for Creative Industries and Innovation, which I now direct.

Thanks to Terry Cutler, Greg Hearn, Mark Ryan, and Michael Keane, co-authors with me of *Research and Innovation Systems in the Production of Digital Content* (CIRAC, QUT and Cutler & Co., 2003), from which some of the policy analysis in the penultimate section was taken. Thanks to Jason Potts, to whom I am indebted for insights on applying evolutionary economic analysis to the Australian creative industries; to Peter Higgs, who has done the hard data-mining yards; to Michael Keane for the update on the China situation, and to John Hartley and Kate Oakley for the same on the United Kingdom.

The author

STUART CUNNINGHAM is Professor of Media and Communications, Queensland University of Technology, and Director of the Australian Research Council Centre of Excellence for Creative Industries and Innovation. He is a key figure in cultural policy studies and is well known for his contributions to media, communications and cultural studies and their relevance to industry practice and government policy. His books include *Featuring Australia* (1991), a study of the pioneering Australian filmmaker Charles Chauvel, and *Framing Culture* (1992), a critique of the limits of cultural studies as applied to cultural policy. He has co-written or co-edited studies of the global dimensions of audiovisual culture and co-authored several major reports for the federal departments of education and communications, the Australian Broadcasting Authority, the Queensland Government and the Brisbane City Council.

He was a board member of the Australian Film Commission in the 1990s, and has spent eight years as foundation chair of QPIX, Queensland's Screen Development Centre. He is Treasurer and Council member of the Australian Academy of the Humanities, a member of the Australian Research Council's College of Experts, and an elected board member of the Council of Humanities, Arts and Social Sciences (CHASS).

1
What is this thing called a creative economy?

Of course, it's the brilliant movies for which our directors, set and fashion designers, cinematographers and actors have received such high international acclaim, marking out Australia as a talent pool of the highest order. It's also the interface designers who have worked in the finance industry to make huge changes in how we do our banking and make investments. This has been one of the most dramatic and rapid changes in mainstream business models seen in a major service sector.

Naturally, it includes our great writers, novelists, playwrights, poets and lyricists, who continue to find ways to reflect back to us our life and times through their exacting and engaging prisms. It's also the 'technical' writer, whose job it is to produce online education and training materials that contribute to Australia's education export successes—Australia's fourth biggest export earner, now worth $6.9 billion to the economy. The film industry earned $2 million from international sales in the same period.

It obviously includes our artists who have made it to the top of tremendously demanding professions and who represent the top echelon of creative talent winnowed through innumerable filters. As Harvard economist Richard E. Caves has written, many hear the call but few survive the round-up.[1] The creative economy is also about the growing legions of amateur and 'pro-am' creatives—bloggers, flash animation mavens, webmeisters—creative and technologically literate *wunderkinder*, who are not minded to wait till the gatekeepers tell them how they can reach an audience.

The creative economy, as we shall see presently, is a hard fish to catch, a difficult category to nail down. But it is bigger and broader than we think, and is much more than culture and the arts. This essay is about why those who support culture and the arts might be interested in the 'creative economy'.

Let me be clear from the outset. This essay is not an argument for or against a better deal for the arts in today's Australia. But I have great sympathy for the idea that far too much negative emphasis is placed on public funding for the arts. In quantum terms, the tax dollar spent on the arts is very small indeed and judicious increases are certainly called for. The Productivity Commission, the government's principal review and advisory body on micro-economic policy and regulation, estimates that Culture and Recreation, the sector where the arts are placed, received less than 1% of its income from the public purse. Compare this to the enormous 14.3% allocated to some manufacturing sectors, and 9.5% to textiles, clothing and footwear. Clearly, the idea that the arts are more heavily subsidised by our hard-earned tax dollar than other sectors is laughable. Thanks to the efforts of excessively influential lobbyists, the amount of corporate welfare routinely thrown at failing industries and mendicant companies is massively greater than that given to the arts. According to the Productivity Commission, tax breaks and handouts that the Federal Government gave to business last year amounted to $4.6 billion.

As John Holden cheekily points out, no-one speaks of the 'subsidised' defence industry, the 'mendicant' education sector or a health system 'propped up' by government funding.[2] Yet all these sectors are funded substantially or wholly by our tax dollars and are subject to the same supposed regime of market failure as the arts and culture. For better and for worse, it is always open season on the arts and culture because they are intimately bound up with controversial inquiries into meaning, purpose and human understanding.

The usual arguments in favour of support for the arts have served us well for a long time. For fifty years or more, cultural economists have given governments good reason to subsidise the arts, with usually bipartisan goodwill. The idea of the cultural industries—the large, mostly commercial, businesses in broadcasting, music and film which deliver popular culture—has given governments reasons to regulate and develop modern cultural policies to support them, and they have done so since the 1960s with a similar commitment. However, the arts now struggle to grow their consumption and support base, while the business models of the cultural industries are facing confronting challenges. The three Ts—technology (the Internet, games and mobile devices), taste (Generations X and Y and the 'millennials' are not into the mass media in the same way as their elders were), and talent (creatively and technologically literate young people are finding other creative channels)—are presenting a formidable challenge to the traditional arguments.

What is urgently needed is a forward-looking view of what a 'creative economy' might look like, and what it might take to strengthen it. It is my contention that fresh arguments and evidence can be found for renewing the case for public investment. Not that this is the only way forward, but it does take up the case on economic grounds, which is where it typically needs to be built in the contemporary policy process.

I want to begin by examining the idea of the 'creative industries' as a broad alliance of activities with creativity at their heart—one that is becoming more central to economic policy and planning, and being entertained seriously in many parts of the world. I will then look at the impact this idea has made in Australia. The subsequent parts of the essay explore the challenges of capturing the full value of the creative industries, particularly when there are so many questions being asked of traditional approaches to culture. I turn then to discuss new economic approaches that might inform the debate, before finally looking at the shape of the policy agendas that are emerging around the culture, creativity and digital content landscape. The 'price' to be paid for a creative economy is that the case for arts and culture will become less about their special or exceptional difference, and become diffused into the need for creativity across the economy and society. To reach our destination, we must take the long way round.

2
The creative industries idea around the world

The idea of creative industries is quite recent.[3] It was developed in the United Kingdom in 1998 by a Creative Industries Taskforce of inter-departmental and industry representatives set up by the incoming Blair Government.[4] The British definition—'activities which have their origin in individual creativity, skill and talent and which have the potential for wealth and job creation through the generation and exploitation of intellectual property'— has remained broadly acceptable world-wide.[5]

It is a definition that encompasses no fewer than thirteen industry sectors: advertising, architecture, arts and antique markets, crafts, design, designer fashion, film, interactive leisure software, music, television and radio, performing arts, publishing and software. Its scope is impressive in its ambitiousness. Indeed, it may be thought too broad to be coherent. At the same time, however, it insists that there is a connection between all thirteen sectors: each has its origin in individual skill, creativity and talent, and each has the potential for wealth and job creation through the exploitation of intellectual property.

When Tony Blair became Prime Minister in 1997, he restructured Britain's Department of Heritage into a Department of Culture, Media and Sport, with the intention of repositioning the UK as 'cool Britannia' for trade and of reasserting its pre-eminence as a creative-industries powerhouse in the world. But there was a further aim, to highlight the value for advanced economies of the fact that the creative industries were already a significant component of GDP, exports and jobs. Indeed, they had been growing at twice the rate of the rest of the economy.

In addition to internal British action in Scotland and the English regions, several other countries have rapidly developed creative-industries strategies.[6] East Asia, Australia and New Zealand are 'hotspots' of these developments.

Korea's approach has seen investment in major infrastructure.[7] The Digital Media City development in Seoul is an attempt to bring together government and corporate infrastructure development and to construct a large cluster of related creative industries in a new precinct. Korean film, TV, games and animation productions are currently riding the crest of the so-called Korean Wave.[8] While Japan built its success predominantly on analog media, Korea has excelled in new media, and is seeing a whole range of renewed creativity flow through the economy. At 75–85% penetration, Korea is significantly ahead of any other country in broadband connectivity. The Korean animation industry, which was organised originally as a low-cost sweatshop for Hollywood animation, is now growing its own indigenous content and films. In general, Korea exhibits all the characteristics at both policy and practice levels of moving well beyond being a Cold War client state of the US.

In the context of a National Development Plan, Taiwan is linking a more 'humanistic and sustainable' approach to development to 'culturally creative industries'.[9] Its goals are to nurture creative skills and promote the combination of culture with entrepreneurship characteristic of the creative industries approach. This necessitates the establishment of a promotional organisation, cultivating a creative workforce for art and design and nurturing design and culture-based industries. There is major new R&D investment in such key areas as design and digital content and incentives to co-operate among industry, academe and research institutions. In the light of a contracting and narrow export industry base, the creative industries are being considered as a way forward. The semi-conductor industry in Taiwan—which is the major export sector and based largely in one area of the country—is considered to be too narrow an export base, particularly with the recent world-wide downturn of the information and communications technology (ICT) sector.

Particular strategies have been implemented in Hong Kong to address the fading eminence of its film and television industries and to reinforce advertising, design, and publishing, aided by a particularly rigorous policy research base.[10] Having invested heavily in ICTs, Singapore now wants to use content and creativity to push the next wave of development beyond its undoubted technocratic excellence.[11] New Zealand has positioned creative industries as one of three key sectors (along with biotechnology and ICT) in its 'growth and innovation framework' that captures the new economy growth strategies.[12] It is a strategy that crisply focuses on the innovative nature of creative design and screen production, boosting the New Zealand brand overseas.

Renewal

There is a view that the creative industries idea might be flavour of the month, and that it will fade along with fashionable rhetoric overhyping other 'sunrise industries'.[13] But there is no evidence yet of that. In fact, two current developments suggest the opposite. One is that it is starting to be taken up in China, the other that it is being strongly refocussed in its original home, the UK.

Creativity is widely understood as embodying distinctive attributes in the arts, in business, technology and the sciences—and also in the broader economy. In China the word for creativity, *chuangyi*, is mostly used in the world of the arts, but also in the advertising, multimedia and design industries. More recently, it has found its way onto educational curricula.

On the other hand, the Chinese term for innovation, *chuangxin*, carries great national freight. Correlations are evident between China's ongoing economic reforms and the national innovation-systems policy, which was officially instituted in 1998 as the 'knowledge innovation program' (*zhishi chuangxin gongcheng*). Accession to the World Trade Organisation in December 2001 signalled a need for broad institutional reform, and, in the eyes of radical reformers, a tide of 'creative destruction' was necessary. Entrepreneurs were admitted into the Chinese Communist Party in 2003.

In January 2006 President Hu Jintao articulated the concept of autonomous innovation (*zizhu chuangxin*).[14] This has led to a broader-based innovation philosophy (*chuangxinxing guojia*). Broadening innovation from its science, engineering and technology base has started to bring to the fore creativity and imagination in other economic and social spheres. We are beginning to see China ready to embrace, or at least accept, creative entrepreneurialism 'from below', while it continues to obey a national imperative imposed 'from above' that it be more industrially and educationally innovative. The economy that is already reshaping geopolitics and economic strategy—and one Australia is formidably dependent on—is already changing from 'made in China' to 'created in China'.[15]

In the United Kingdom, after almost ten years, two major reviews and a political makeover have refocused the creative industries idea and a dedicated junior minister's portfolio has been created within the Department of Culture, Media and Sport. This is the responsibility of James Purnell who, as Minister for the Creative Industries and Tourism, has instituted a Creative Economy Programme,[16] which is refocusing creative industries towards higher growth business development and clearer differentiations of economic and cultural goals. Major national reviews this year have recommended creativity/innovation 'centres of excellence' in all regions and a close look at the whole canvas of intellectual property law as a precondition for a healthy knowledge-based society and economy. An ancillary development is the further embedding of the idea in higher education and training. Indeed, several universities are currently expanding their 'creative industries' portfolios and advertising professorships in the field.

London has built one of the most rigorous evidence bases for the importance of the creative industries. It shows that creative industries are second only to business services in driving the London economy. The industry represents the second largest sector employer, with 600,000 people working either directly in creative industries or in creative occupations in other industries. They contribute more than 4% of Britain's export income and provide jobs for over two million people.[17] Estimates put the world market at over $3.04 trillion in 2005, a figure that may have doubled by 2020.[18]

These are data to die for. But what about the situation in Australia?

3
The situation in Australia

The creative industries idea has been in play in Australia since the late 1990s. It was preceded by an intense period of policy thought represented by *Commerce in Content*, *The Online Economy*, *Excellence in Content*, the Broadband Services Expert group (BSEG) reports and, of course, *Creative Nation* in the mid-1990s.[19] While current policy formulation has yet to translate into significant federal government action, the level of activity shows that this sector is more visible on Canberra's radar now than at any time since the mid-1990s.[20]

Since 2001, there has been a comprehensive Creative Industries Cluster Study, a Digital Content Industry Action Agenda, a Prime Minister's Science, Engineering and Innovation Council inquiry into 'Creativity in the Information Economy' and a Creative Innovation Strategy from the Australia Council.[21] What we are seeing is the development of an innovation framework appropriate for creative content The focus has shifted towards the 'digital content and applications' aspect of the creative industries, and raised a greater understanding that creative industries *outputs* and creative occupations are becoming a more important *input* into manufacturing and the wider service industries, such as health, education, government and business services.

In 2001, Senator Richard Alston, at the time Federal Minister for Communications, IT and the Arts, inaugurated the Creative Industries Cluster Study (CICS). And it is CICS that, at a national level, has seen a shift from a cultural policy framework to an industry policy framework. This change in approach views the creative and digital content industries more in terms of industry policy than purely arts or cultural policy. The various reports in the CICS examined the agglomeration characteristics of creative industries. It considered company structure and performance, particularly issues of fragmentation in the industry. It also examined export issues, broadband infrastructure and the role of cultural institutions in facilitating industry development. One of the reports—entitled

'Research and innovation systems in the production of Digital Content and Applications' and written by Cutler & Company and a Queensland University of Technology (QUT) team—applied, for the first time, an innovation systems approach to building the digital content and creative industries. I shall look at this in greater detail in section 8.

Queensland took some innovative action: the State Government teamed with QUT to build a $60 million Creative Industries Precinct. Seeking to make the creative industries idea a physical reality, this project brought together on a single site, higher education, R&D, creative businesses, arts and new media display and exhibition. In operation since 2004, the precinct houses most of the Creative Industries Faculty's staff and students, plus their facilities; eleven small and medium-sized creative enterprises; a company promoting business links with creative talent and research capacity; a professional theatre company (La Boite and the Roundhouse Theatre); Australia's only Co-operative Research Centre in interaction design and an ARC Centre of Excellence in Creative Industries and Innovation, the only such centre outside the sciences. The Queensland Government has built on this, producing a splashy creative industries strategy, *Creativity is Big Business*.[22]

The most recent national initiatives have been a Prime Minister's Science, Engineering and Innovation Council (PMSEIC) inquiry into 'Creativity in the Information Economy', which was held in 2005, and a Digital Content Industry Action Agenda, released in March 2006. The recommendations of the PMSEIC inquiry included the establishment of a local version of the UK's National Endowment for Science, Technology and the Arts (NESTA), in order to develop better cross-disciplinary educational opportunities, and to extend the country's heavy investment in science and innovation so as to include creativity and the creative industries. The Digital Content Industry Action Agenda has been devised to double the value of the digital content industry to the Australian economy, to a total of $42 billion by 2015. Its recommendations are aimed at improving private investment in the sector by such strategies as the development of stronger export performance, the strengthening of links between industry and the providers of skills and training and R&D institutions; and by ensuring that intellectual property regimes keep pace with technological and social change. The Agenda also wants much better sources of timely data that can inform planning by both industry and government.

The Australia Council's Creative Innovation Strategy seeks to capture these policy trends for the creative community it serves.[23] The term 'creative innovation' itself makes the point that what the sciences call *innovation* the arts and humanities call *creativity*—so, to align the two is to urge stronger links between what are otherwise thought to be disparate sectors. The new strategy shows the Council to be reaching out to forge formal and informal partnerships with R&D centres, industry players and artists' peak bodies, and demonstrates its determination to be a contributor to contemporary innovation policy.

4
Why is this important? From creative *industries* to creative *economy*

As we have seen, the creative industries idea has gained wide purchase in contemporary policy and industry debate, its proponents seeking to reshape relations between old and new media and the cultural sector; and to reposition media, communications and culture as a driver, rather than a passenger, in the knowledge economy. Their further aim is to connect the sector to national innovation agendas and thereby move it into the sphere of research-based, knowledge-intensive industry policy. What defines creative industries in the economy is the proposition that 'creativity' is their *primary* source of value, something that is becoming increasingly important for growth in post-industrial, knowledge-based societies. In other words, the aim is to foreground the sector's economic potential and make the creative industries the 'spark-plugs' of next generation, post-industrial growth.[24]

A creative industries approach brings together a range of sectors which have not hitherto been linked and thus it has expanded greatly the domain of what is typically counted, throwing settled categories like arts, media, culture, and cultural industries into a more dynamic process. To give one, admittedly extreme, example, John Howkins defines the creative economy as simply 'financial transactions in creative products', whose economic value is secured through copyright, design, trademark and patents, and therefore includes the sciences, engineering and technology (SET) sectors along with the arts, media, new media, design and architecture.[25] On this basis, the creative economy in 1999 accounted for $US2.2 trillion, or about 7.3% of the global economy. The contribution of the creative and performing arts, however, a mere 1.7% of this total, has shrunk to virtual insignificance. Apart from science R&D, which massively—and, in my view, undeservedly—expands the economic quantum of the sector, the real powerhouses are publishing, software and broadcasting.

Furthermore, the sectors within creative industries—the established arts (theatre, dance, music, visual arts), the established media (radio, film, TV), the large design and architecture sectors, and new media (software, games, e-commerce and mobile content)—range from the resolutely non-commercial to the high-tech and commercial. It is also a spectrum that encompasses not only the culturally- and often location-specific, but also the globalised and generically creative, inviting such questions as how creative inputs drive wider industry sectors, and how sectors with very different business models, revenue sources, demand drivers and scale and purpose, can co-exist productively elsewhere than in a policy-maker's dream.

This continuum is less coherent than our traditional, neat definitions of the arts, media and cultural industries, but more dynamic and relevant to contemporary policy-making. One reason why the idea of creative industries has been taken up widely is that it connects two key contemporary policy clusters: on the one hand, elements of the high-growth ICT and R&D-based *production in the new economy* and, on the other, those types of *consumption in the new economy* redolent of cultural identity and social empowerment. Critics of the creative industries idea are fearful that, by introducing into the rationale for supporting culture too great an emphasis on economics, it might marginalise the traditional arts sectors. However, the benefits of mainstreaming culture and media into policy powerhouses of industry development and innovation arguably outweigh the drawbacks.

We need to understand better the full dimensions of the creative industries as there is a tendency to systematically underestimate their size and economic impact in official counts. But we need also to move from an emphasis on understanding creative *outputs* (culture) to creative *inputs* into the wider economy. Much of the real growth dynamics will be found in this move. The creative *industries* constitute one sector of the economy; the creative *economy* is formed when we move from sector-specific arguments to creative occupations as inputs into the whole economy, and creative outputs as intermediate inputs into other sectors. Indeed, the central aim of the present essay is to urge that, mindful of the example of ICTs in recent decades, we acknowledge that creativity too has the potential to be a powerful enabler of economic growth.

This takes us into territory recently investigated by Richard Florida, who, instead of analysing industry sectors, concentrates on occupational statistics in order to measure a city's or a region's potential for, or success as, a creative 'hotspot'.[26] While Florida's work may be open to criticism, it is undeniable that his focus on *occupation* and *qualification* counterbalances the usual dependence simply on *industry* statistics in industry development debates. To stress occupation statistics and the place of the creative industries in the wider economy is tantamount to saying that creative skills have become economically significant, and are growing in value to the broader economy.

Florida's work on the 'creative class' has highlighted the wider economic significance of creative human capital, especially in underpinning high technology industry development. The following 'creativity index', prepared in 2002 by National Economics, compares Australia and the United States in terms of population diversity, high-tech output, innovation and human capital.[27]

TABLE 1

Creativity index: Top ten regions (Australia and USA)

AUSTRALIA	SCORE	USA	SCORE
Global Sydney	992	San Francisco	1057
Melbourne Inner	985	Austin	1028
ACT	831	San Diego	1015
Perth Central	744	Boston	1015
Adelaide Central	735	Seattle	1008
Sydney Inner West	733	Raleigh-Durham	996
Brisbane City	720	Houston	980
Melbourne South	606	Washington-Baltimore	964
Sydney Outer North	535	New York	962
Melbourne East	519	Dallas	960

It shows that if Sydney and Melbourne were ranked among US cities they would be in seventh and eighth positions respectively.

Further comparison indicates that, as a percentage of the population, the US's 'super creatives' (Florida's term for the core of the class) outrank Australia's by approximately two percentage points. However, the reverse holds for the second-tier creative professionals in business services, health and education, in which sector Australia is superior. Australia also out-performs the US on both Florida's Bohemian Index of arts workers as a proportion of population, and on his Diversity Index (which measures cultural and lifestyle diversity). The areas in which we lag significantly are innovation (patents per capita), human capital talent (the percentage of the population with a higher degree) and high technology production.

While National Economics' Australian survey confirms and replicates the US findings of Richard Florida regarding the correlation between concentrations of creative populations and the location of high tech industries, it is also apparent that Australia is not levering its creative capital with economic outcomes as successfully as the US. This suggests that there are significant points of failure in Australia's national innovation system.

Recent work, conducted by the ARC Centre of Excellence for Creative Industries and Innovation, with new field research and substantial data-gathering and data-mining tries to take this analysis forward.[28] Evidence from our research projects, *Mapping Queensland's Creative Industries* and *Creative Digital Industries in Australia*, demonstrate that these sectors are significantly underestimated in official statistics whose categories lag badly behind the growth of, particularly, the digital end of this industry sector. We have refined official categories into which the data fits in a way that reflects the changing realities of these industry sectors. We have also counted much more comprehensively the economic contributions of creative people and organisations by correlating industry sector with occupation.

Most mapping studies have naturally been focused on industries and therefore gathered data about the specialist firms operating within each specific segment. But measuring the creative 'impact' on the economy needs to encompass both specialist creative *industries* activity and the breadth of specialist creative *occupations*. There is frequent movement between these types of activity. For example, an individual might operate solo as an independent film producer, and then move to work for a government film agency; or else an independent designer might sign a three-year contract to work for a bank or advertising agency.

The direct economic impact of creative industries has been significantly under-estimated. For example, our analysis has shown that, because so many designers are embedded in other industries and because design is defined and counted in such an unhelpful way, the design sector is undercounted by some 36%.

Design consulting activities are often subsumed into much broader business services, or technical services, or even clothing manufacturing classifications. And when specialist occupations *are* tallied, the failure to take into account the support and management staff that work within specialist creative firms still

TABLE 2
Total Australian employment within the creative trident
(Census, 2001)

I N D U S T R Y

	Employment within creative industries	Employment within other industries	Total employed
Employed in core creative occupations	Specialist: 138,623	Embedded: 159,476	298,099
Employed in other occupations	Support: 147,891		147,891
Total employed	286,514	159,476	445,990

O C C U P A T I O N

results in total employment being underestimated by as much as 33%.

We have dubbed measurement of all three axes the 'creative trident', which is the total of: creative occupations within the creative industries ('specialist'), plus the creative occupations employed in *other* industries ('embedded'), plus the *support* occupations employed in creative industries.

This means that 138,623 people were employed in creative occupations within the *core* creative industries, another 159,476 in creative occupations within *other* industries, and a further 147,891 in *support, managerial* or *sales* occupations within specialist creative industries. People who are 'embedded', i.e. employed in creative occupations outside of specific creative industries, and are spread across all industry divisions, constitute almost 2% of the total Australian workforce.

Total trident employment amounted to almost 446,000 people in Australia in 2001, which is substantially higher than the estimated employment figure of 211,638 used in the 2003 *Creative Industries Cluster Study: Cottages to Corporations Report* and 100,000 higher than the estimate of 345,000 used in the 2002 *Creative Industries Cluster Study: Stage One Report.*[29] The *Stage One Report* included employment in related industries, such as distribution. Based on their earnings as recorded in the census, the people employed made an annual contribution in wages and salaries of over $21 billion directly to the Australian economy.

Apart from this revaluation of the quantum of creative people and activity in our economy, there are other important pointers to a different profile for the sector that have been produced from this research. The Creative Trident represents approximately 5.5% of Australian employment, 5% of GST-paying enterprises and 8% of non-GST-paying enterprises. These percentages are all markedly higher than those given in standard statistical analyses. Our detailed work on *The Ecology of Queensland Design* is one of many international studies which focus on the input value of the design occupation. Design is one of the leading examples of creative inputs into the broader economy, including, and especially, manufacturing.[30] We found that the 'Creative Trident' for design activity in Queensland resulted in a count of twice that of standard statistical analyses.

The whole sector has a mean income 34% higher than the economy as a whole, which suggests a different profile for creatives than the more widespread understanding of a low-wage, high-volunteer sector. In the Queensland study, we found that exports and gross value added are higher than average sectorally, and that creative industries tend to be more knowledge-intensive in that they spend more on knowledge-based workers as a percentage of their total wages spend than other sectors.

These findings are suggestive rather than definitive, but they do provide pointers in the direction of the movement from a sector-specific to an economy-wide focus. Just as the ICT sector benefited from the input-value it was shown to afford the economy as a whole, so the data suggests that a similar value can begin to be seen with creative inputs.

5
Shifting policy rationales, shifting economics

The established economic approaches to culture and the arts may have been thrown a curveball by the notions of creative industries and economy. However, creative-industries theory, analysis and policy have a way to go before they establish a robust economic framework that compellingly captures the value of the creative sector and thereby might provide fresh rationale for public support for the sector. It must first engage with cultural economics, that established sub-branch of neo-classical economics, and then with the economic thinking that underlies the concept of the 'cultural industries'.

Cultural economics analyses largely settled industry sectors and focuses on microeconomic analysis of choice in established markets. It concentrates on the exceptional character of these markets or quasi-markets which is held to be due to the unusual nature of choice and decision-making by both suppliers and purchasers in these markets. The traditional approach to the arts and culture employs an argument for public support based on 'exceptional' economic activity in which there will always be market failure.

Cultural economics has typically focused on the arts end of the creative industries spectrum, often because these arguments and assumptions work best at that end. David Throsby is Australia's foremost exponent of cultural economics. In *Economics and Culture*, his most comprehensive exposition of his position, he builds in a working assumption that 'the creative arts as traditionally defined' are the core sectors in a cultural industry model because they are the 'locus of origin of creative ideas'.[31] Throsby reiterates this argument in his recent Platform Paper,[32] where he argues that a flourishing arts sector is 'one of the most enduring foundations' on which to build the cultural industries.

This notion, while often seen and adopted in various forms, conflates static and dynamic models of economic analysis in that it assumes that, because some sectors have more creatives as a proportion of the whole workforce in that sector, they must be the 'locus of origin of creative ideas'. Also built into the model is the dubious assumption that the more sectors produce both cultural and non-cultural goods and services (such as the large industrialised creative industries), the less 'core' they are. Given the capacity for 'creative ideas' to diffuse further when they are embedded into other products and services, and given the data that shows that more creatives are found in other industry sectors than in specialist sectors, I would have thought the opposite was a more interesting hypothesis. The sources of innovation propelled by creatives will be found across the creative industries and increasingly across the wider economy. The 'enduring foundation' lies more where creative qualifications and occupations are deployed than in particular output/industry sectors. (Of the total population with 'creative' qualifications at the last census, we estimate that about 70% of those employed were working outside the specialist creative industries.) This suggests a human capital model, rather than an 'exceptional sector' model, for the importance of creativity in the economy.

The foundations of public support for the cultural industries—the large, mostly commercial, businesses in broadcasting, music and film, which deliver popular culture—are somewhat more complex. They lie in a combination of cultural sovereignty, market failure and natural monopoly/oligopoly. The cultural sovereignty part asserts that it is important to project Australian content into those media where most Australians are consuming their culture. But imported content is much cheaper to buy and comes with inbuilt publicity and momentum. Thus, the local product needs support to level the playing field, as it were. This is the market failure part which justifies public investment. The need for content regulations which require commercial radio and television to broadcast certain amounts of Australian product is a variation on the natural monopoly argument. Broadcasters enjoy very significant protection from competition because they use a scarce public resource, the electromagnetic spectrum. The quid pro quo for this 'natural oligopoly' is the cultural dividend extracted through content regulation.

In fact, the cultural rationale for content regulation has a generally unacknowledged weakness. Most television transmission quota regulations are based on a broad, generic cultural remit: that national culture is represented by whatever content is found on television. This is an *anthropological* account of culture. But regulation for specific forms of television, such as expensive fictional drama and social documentary, is based on cultural exceptionalism. According to the official argument, fictional drama is a crucial genre in our national culture, because it narrates, heightens and dramatises national stories, while also providing crucial alternatives to US dominance. The official argument has to be of this more intense nature—*culture as art*—because such content may not be produced without state intervention. The rationale then becomes one of market failure to provide such expensive programming, because of its cost relative to imported content.

However, with emerging evidence that there is a decline in audience demand for high-budget series and one-off TV dramas, the market failure argument is weakened, and specifically-cultural policy for television is no longer based on a popular cultural mandate, but is pushed back to more of an 'arts and audience development' strategy. Is the trend away from nation-defining drama to reality TV, from authored texts to branded experiences, a cultural, generational shift? Or has it to do with the corporate strategies of the television industry driving unit costs of content creation inexorably down in the face of the exploding multi-channel marketplace and the fragmentation of the audience base? While the latter is undoubtedly the case, it is too early to say whether the former, the cultural shift, is irreversible.

Such endogenous challenges to the regulatory settlement are now more than matched by exogenous change. These include shifts in what might count as popular culture (as we shall see in the next section) as well as a *deus ex machina* such as the Australia-United States Free Trade Agreement. The FTA has effectively capped such initiatives as government might take to extend content regulation and even public investment into emerging new media environments.

Before looking at versions of economics which we might use to understand the emerging creative economy, we need to consider the rationale for investment in public-service broadcasting—the ABC and SBS—which is by far the largest single outlay for cultural industries in this country.

Government appropriation to the ABC (about $800m per annum) is more than six times larger than that to the Australia Council. Its position in the bustling marketplace of popular culture is under significantly greater threat than that of bodies which enjoy basically bipartisan political support and are usually at the margins of governments' financial radar. It is not for nothing that the ABC is often claimed to be Australia's most important cultural institution: it potentially links modernist culture (nation-building, linking regional and rural with the cities; its education and arts remit; the centrality of news and current affairs) with the post-modern, with innovative technology and creative R&D, and not least with artists' career development—and all this under a charter which retains the essence of public service in the best, traditional sense. It has distributional muscle and has shown it can lead in innovation (ABC Online); it can bring broad-based content to the people; it can break out of the inner-city latte belt. That it is under continuing attack is a sign of the ABC's enduring importance in the Australian polity and culture.

We need economists here, because the tried-and-tested argument for government action around culture—market failure—doesn't apply at all neatly to public-service broadcasting (PSB). The ABC and SBS operate in an abundant marketplace that does not lack for any of the program formats produced by these broadcasters. PSB's core *raison d'être* is not market failure, but is more complex and important. It is to be found in its complex of nation-building (or nation-maintaining) roles: delivering key information and news and current affairs unburdened by commercial interests and thus performing a key informal educative function (thus maintaining a 'trust' relationship in a 'risk' society); and providing essential R&D into the Australian cultural landscape by being able to innovate, take risks, and connect creative people to a broad-based audience. That it is not doing much of this well at the moment—due to relentless attacks, financial starvation and being placed at the nerve-centre of the culture wars—is cause for the highest priority concern. The economics that might help to secure the future for public-service broadcasting would be focused not only on efficiency or market failure but on its role in innovation.[33]

6

The culture, it is a-changin'

Looking ahead, what are some of the key emergent cultural practices in the twenty-first century? What is likely to gain ground and drive innovation? Consumption drives post-industrial economies more and more, and its nature is changing. More and more consumer activity around media and culture is do-it-yourself, user-generated content. There is huge growth in peer-to-peer activity and a more 'participatory' culture. Some of the neologisms that capture this phenomenon blur the lines between production and consumption: there is now 'prosumption', engaged in by 'produsers'.

There is more user-generated content on the Internet than professionally-produced and corporate content. User-led innovations, such as SMS, have changed the business model for mobile devices, one of the most dynamic growth-sectors of the economy, leading to successful MMS (picture cameras) uptake and heavy R&D and investment in mobile content, which in turn has led to expanding opportunities for creatives.

There is the Wikipedia for knowledge production, Meetup and MyPlace for civic formation, OhMyNews for citizen journalism, Orion's Arm—an online science-fiction, world-building project for identity formation—and Amazon and eBay Web Services for independent market advice. Twenty-five per cent of all Internet users in the US are also blog readers. There is Digital Storytelling, where all those with life stories, but no prior access to media technologies, can engage in a process of releasing those stories—in the case of the world-leading practice in the Capture Wales program, onto BBC TV and websites, a form of vernacular literacy in which virtually anyone can participate.

There's Flash, the animation software which is virtually ubiquitous on networked computers as an enabling platform for global vernacular creativity. And there's Current TV (www.current.tv). This is not much like in mainstream TV—at least, not yet! Launched in the US in mid-2005, already about a quarter of its airtime is user-generated and it publishes some of the best DIY production guides for viewers to become 'produsers'.

Of course, we might get carried away with user-led innovation. Might it not go the way of the dotcom bubble? Is it not just another of those new media 'moments' which always seem to promise revolution—the Internet as the end of social dislocation and hierarchical media relations, TV as the world's demotic educator, and so on? But when, in his 2005 address to the American Society of Newspaper Editors, Rupert Murdoch starts talking about digital 'natives' and 'immigrants' and acknowledges that News Corp has underestimated the impact of Internet-based news sourcing and the social logic or 'collective intelligence'—not to mention the impact on the bottom line—of peer-to-peer communication, then, as Eric Beecher surmised recently, 'Something seismic is going on. Seismic, but unpredictable.'[34] Reputedly, Murdoch was scared into this position by data such as those presented by the Carnegie Foundation, demonstrating that 'new forms of newsgathering and distribution, grassroots or citizen journalism and blogging sites are changing the very nature of who produces news' and that the 18–34 demographic is creating this inexorable momentum.[35]

What are the deep implications of this new take on culture? First, it disrupts the linear value chain of professional modes of production. Secondly, the innovations are as much about distribution as production.

One way to understand this emergent paradigm shift is to consider Richard Caves' brilliant summary of the 'Basic Economic Properties of Creative Activities' that constitute the mainstream arts and media today—and then consider how they need to change in order to deal with 'future culture':

1. 'Nobody knows'/demand is uncertain. (There is radical uncertainty about the likely demand

for creative product, due to the fact that such products are 'experience goods', about which buyers lack information prior to consumption, and the satisfaction derived is largely subjective and intangible.)

2. 'Art for arts sake'/creative workers care about their product. (Creative producers derive substantial non-economic forms of satisfaction from their work. This makes them vulnerable to exploitation and to supply almost always outstripping demand, thus fundamentally distorting market equilibrium.)

3. 'Motley crew'/some products require diverse skills. (Creative production is mostly collective in nature. Hence the need to develop and maintain creative teams that have diverse skills, and often also diverse interests and expectations about the final product.)

4. 'Infinite variety'/differentiated products. (There is a huge variety of creative products available, both within particular formats (rental-store videos, for example) and between formats. Each creative output is to a greater or lesser extent a prototype of itself, and thus as much or more effort has to go into marketing as production, if it is to stand a chance for success.)

5. 'A-list/B-list'/vertically-differentiated skills. (All creative sectors display great difference between the bright stars and the 'long tail' and this plays out in both remuneration and recognition, and also in the ways in which producers or other content aggregators rank and assess creative personnel.)

6. 'Time flies'/time is of the essence. (Most industrial forms of creative production need to co-ordinate diverse creative activities within short time-frames.)

7. 'Ars longa'/durable products and durable rents. (Many cultural products have great durability, their producers having the capacity to continue extracting economic rents (for example, copyright payments) long after the period of production.)[36]

Of these principles, at least four must be rethought in the light of 'produsers', 'prosumption' and user-generated content. The vast gap between the famous few and the long tail ('A-list/B-list/vertically-differentiated skills') is radically challenged. There is competition for recognition, and often a desire for commercial success, but participatory culture is a much more level playing field. 'Nobody knows/demand is uncertain' is turned on its head as supply is starting to come from the demand side. 'Art for arts sake/creative workers care about their product' will continue, but with a possible vengeance as their care about their product may be translated into a lesser willingness to accept the asymmetrical contracts which place most risk and most profit in the hands of the mainstream aggregator. 'Infinite variety/differentiated products' becomes less a major obstacle to effective and cost-efficient marketing and to risk management than a challenge to find enough 'market' bits to make low cost, low entry production and distribution viable. The growing confidence of models for independent distribution of creative content see the Internet as having unique potential for constituting newly viable markets.

7
Emerging varieties of economics

By contrast to the static reallocation model of cultural economics, an economics which captures the dimensions and trends in the creative economy needs to be dynamic, focusing on sources of novelty and change and on both the way industries grow (rather than their size at any one particular moment in time) and what drives them to grow. Much of this novelty and change may increasingly be found in the demand rather than the supply side of the equation, if the previous section's argument tells us anything. Analysis may also be redirected, away from resource allocation arguments and towards the way/s in which the creative industries function as a bell-wether for structural change in modern economies. Several bodies of economic thought need to be tapped to engage this challenge, among them transaction-cost economics, growth theory, and evolutionary and information economics. This process has only begun.

Examples of this kind of work applied to the economics of creative industries have sought to steer economic analysis in some interesting and *prima facie* surprising new directions. The first of these analysed information imperfections and asymmetries in agents and markets under the heading of the new information economics and the modern transactions cost theory of organisations. The best example of this—indeed, a definitive work on the organisation of the arts industries—is Richard Caves' *Creative Industries*, which uses transactions-cost theory developed in the 1970s to explain the logic of the complex, time-dependent contracts and organisational forms in an industry characterised by extreme uncertainty and highly mobile factors of production. The transaction-cost approach highlighted the fact that the creative industries were exceptional, less in their cultural goods aspects than in the evolution of highly-complex contractual forms and their ability to live in a rapidly-changing market environment through the constant production of novelty.

This line of work has been further developed by Arthur De Vany in his *Hollywood Economics: How Extreme Uncertainty Shapes the Film Industry*, which uses complexity theory from the late 1980s to show how the pattern of economic outcomes of firms and cultural products like movies conforms to the characteristic power-law signatures that are ubiquitous in evolutionary processes.[37] (Power-law signatures include the long tail, the 'A-list/B-list' phenomenon, and very high rates of company entry and exit from the industry.) Again, this reinforces the message that the economics of creative industries might be understood in terms of their complex industrial and enterprise dynamics and their similarity to the high-tech end of the economy. Both Caves and De Vany provide fresh insight into the dynamic structure of the arts industries and the way/s in which markets and organisations cope with the volatility inherent in this industry.

Over the last ten years a new, 'evolutionary' approach to economic analysis has taken shape, which places particular focus on the dynamics of the economic system under conditions of variety generation, enterprise competition and selection and self-organisation. Stan Metcalfe, Brian Loasby and Jason Potts have all published readable accounts of these developments.[38] Most of the empirical and theoretical work so far undertaken in modern evolutionary economics has focused on manufacturing and high technology sectors, as have most analyses of the sources of innovation in contemporary economies. Unfortunately, there is little yet that seeks to apply this new framework to the economic analysis of creative industries, although some of the most interesting is focused on the broader question of innovation in services.[39] The core advance that this approach might facilitate is to understand creative industries as an emergent, innovative part of the services sector of the economy, rather than presenting them as an exception to mainstream industries, as 'not just another business'. The professional interest group Focus on Creative Industries (FOCI) in the UK captured this well:

> Whilst FOCI welcomes the recognition of the strong economic contribution made by the creative industries in terms of wealth creation and employment, we would also keenly stress that this sector is very different from traditional industries. They deal in value and values, signs and symbols; they are multi-skilled and fluid; they move between niches and create hybrids; they are multi-national and they thrive on the margins of economic activity; they mix up making money and making meaning. The challenge of the creative industries is the challenge of a new form of

economic understanding—they are not 'catching up' with serious, mainstream industries, they are setting the templates which these industries will follow.[40]

The evolutionary approach places a focus on the ways economies *grow*, as complex open systems, rather than by optimising allocative efficiencies. It is also offers a clearer understanding of the way in which new technologies are integrated into an economy and the restructuring of organisations, industries, markets and consumer lifestyles the evolutionary growth process requires. The creative industries' complex contractual and organisational structures, inherent uncertainty, power-law revenue streams, and high rates of experimentation—not unlike some of Caves' 'basic economic properties of creative activities'—suggest that they may be 'pure' cases of service-based competitive enterprise in a fundamentally uncertain environment.

Evolutionary economics may therefore hope to provide a new basis for assessing the significance of the creative industries by focusing analytic attention on how the industry is dynamically structured and how it changes. This may furnish us with a clearer view of how it is able to adapt to change and explore niches available to it, as well as how it feeds variety into the economic system that other industries and sectors can further exploit. We are seeking to better understand the organisational, market and industrial dynamics of how the creative industries grow and change, as well as the effect this has on the dynamics of other parts of the economy. We shall be particularly interested to see how the creative industries integrate and transform new technologies into new services and how variety in the economy is regenerated by the continuous flows of novelty (in content or design, for example) into all parts of the economy.

The value of such novelty or variety is negligible in a static analysis, but from the dynamic perspective it is grist to the mill of economic growth and evolution. To properly understand their role, the creative industries need to be evaluated in terms of the way in which they both induce and facilitate the ongoing process of economic transformation. For the discipline of economics, this is where their true value might lie, not in appeals 'beyond the market' to notions of un-revealed preferences or cultural value.

Compare this approach to the types of evidence presented earlier from the QUT creative industries mapping analyses. This time the focus would not be on the size of the sector but on indicators of how the creative industries inject dynamic influences into the economy. For example, why is design important? One might say that aesthetic values are important, or that in an enterprise economy—in which all firms must continually introduce new and better goods and services just to stay in the market—good design provides a competitive edge in better performance and in attracting the consumer's attention. Design, however, is irrelevant in a static economy, because nothing new is ever being introduced and firms are not competing in this manner of rivalry and enterprise. The value of design will always be highest in an innovation-driven, enterprise economy. A further example: why is user-originated content and user-led innovation important? It's not necessarily the size of the sector—games are bigger than film; there is more user-generated content on the Internet than professionally-produced and corporate content, and so on—though that indicates something significant. It's that they provide a classic instance of 'creative destruction', upsetting the business models of the established communications conglomerates, introducing novelty into the system, and leading even Rupert Murdoch himself to presage the end of the days of the media mogul.

Evolutionary analysis also defines why it is so hard to capture the creative industries within standard classification systems such as our ANZSICs, the Australian and New Zealand Standard Industry Classifications. The classification crisis is itself evidence of a sector that is rapidly changing and subject to greater and greater differentiation and specialisation. This is the hallmark of what evolutionary economics would call the *growth* of knowledge—the hallmark of a knowledge-based economy. Inside these classification conundrums lies the disruptive emergence of many new species of industry.

8
What is to be done?

If we accept that creative industries may benefit from being positioned less in the realm of cultural policy and more towards the idea of creativity as an input into the broader economy and towards the knowledge-intensive dimensions driving innovation and change, a raft of policy domains and programs comes into play. There are implications for education and R&D policy, innovation policy, including export, tax, intellectual property as well as cultural policy. (Bringing these into better alignment is the goal of the new Australian Research Council Centre of Excellence for Creative Industries and Innovation, which I direct.) It is a great challenge for governments and industry to deliver joined-up initiatives to support holistic or systemic approaches. And the amount of activity is not the only issue; it is also and equally about co-ordination, getting the linkages working better.

As we have seen in section 3, there have been many policy recommendations made recently which I do not propose to rehearse here. Instead, I will draw on the substantial analysis conducted recently by Cutler and Company and a Queensland University of Technology team, that applied, uniquely for Australia, an innovation systems approach to building the digital content and creative industries.[41]

There are many *elements* of an innovation and industry development system in place. We have a very large education and training sector producing skilled graduates and trainees. We have large market organisers and industry players, both in the public sector (broadcasters, funding agencies, and cultural institutions such as museums and galleries) and in the private sector (commercial broadcasters, publishing houses, telecommunications firms, and advertising). There is strong and growing demand for such a system, both in retail consumer demand and in the role of digital content as an enabler across a growing range of industries, particularly in the services and manufacturing sector.

However, the *quality of linkages* and the *lack of clear public policy signals and frameworks*, together with a number of other critical issues, mark the innovation system as, at best, embryonic. Public policy needs to address the shifts required to capture the innovation potential of digital content industries by moving, for example, from unrelated cultural and higher education policies to a more dynamic mix of coordinated program initiatives.

Several strategies exist to improve the situation. A Digital Content Industry Action Agenda has been developed to establish a framework for alignment of existing policy regimes with digital content industries. A primary focus of the innovation agenda must be to better align cultural policies with industry development and R&D policies. What are needed now are nationally-funded centres of research to promote university and industry linkages that will establish *tripartite* interfaces between cultural institutions, universities and content industries. Such an initiative would create incentives for, and legitimise the role of, cultural institutions in research collaborations. Such an R&D initiative might invite a levy from participating industry sectors to fund innovation, which would then trigger government funding. This is the model adopted by many established R&D boards for primary industries. The industry levy might apply to broadcasters, publishers and distributors, and could be limited to firms with turnover above a floor level, to exempt emerging small- and medium-sized enterprises. Levy contributions could also offset, or replace, some or all existing broadcasting licence and other imposts. In the event of any major changes to cross-media or ownership rules, the scheme could be extended to offset any windback of existing local production requirements. An essential element of such a centre (or R&D corporation) would be a national information and resource brokerage centre for the sector to address the serious and endemic information asymmetries and structural weakness in the innovation system.

Equally necessary is a suite of reforms to research, and higher education policies to accommodate, digital content and the creative industries; including campaigns targeting young people with the message that knowledge entrepreneurship—a 'creative career'—is a viable and attractive option. Supporting and promoting export is important as the only way to sustainable growth. Equally important is the fact that only hard evidence of sustainability and scalability will make the sector attractive to private investors and break the vicious cycle of underinvestment.

The role of broadcasting and broadband in the innovation system is crucial, as the gateway between established and emergent *content creation* (popular media's migration to interactivity and mass customisation) and *industry structure* (from highly centralized distributional models to more networked and distributed models). Understanding the interaction between the potent legacy of broadcasting and the potential of convergent broadband media is the key, if content creation is to remain close to the mainstream of popular cultural consumption and not be siphoned off into science or art alone.

Major technology-related reforms include national investment in content and metadata standards and supporting systems, thus limiting the huge transaction costs for both producers and users created by the current 'bottom up' approach to standards. They also include tax credits for R&D investment in technology infrastructure in emerging content areas. Both are crucial missing pieces in the innovation jigsaw.

Open content repositories, or public domain digital content, are the content industries equivalent of open source software. They *selectively* address barriers to production and unintended cultural outcomes of prevailing copyright and intellectual property regimes through an alternative *opt-in* model which can operate in parallel with existing regimes. As such it can be a powerful structural mechanism to support a rich 'digital sand pit' for creative content producers. The measure facilitates the active re-directing and re-use of digital content assets. Misuse of this public domain material would be protected under the provisions of a general non-exclusive Public Licence scheme.

In short, an innovation systems approach to the creative industries opens up central policy territory which, until now, has been the preserve of science, engineering and technology. It seeks to move culture into mainstream policy calculation by connecting culture to the most trenchant current rationale for active government involvement in industry shaping.

9
What price a creative economy?

There are, and will be, plenty of critics of this line of argument about the creative industries and a creative economy. They do, and will, worry that it might marginalise the traditional arts sectors and introduce an untoward economism into rationales for support for culture. It will be said that if we put our faith in economic data, we are sure to fail, as we argue on 'their' turf. John Holden, for one, argues for a return to 'intrinsic' justifications for the arts as a way of solving their 'crisis of legitimacy'.[42] I am attracted to the proposition that policy should be fashioned from the self-understanding of creative people, but the critical spirit that constitutes the creative community makes me doubt that there would be a robust and enduring consensus about what an 'intrinsic' justification is. Would it be strong enough to withstand the processes that contemporary public funding must go through? What is intrinsically important about culture? *Pour épater le bourgeois*? Indigenous social laws and beliefs? Aesthetic excellence before all else? National projection? A good night out?

And there is always the flip side to intrinsic arguments stating the essential benefits that flow from culture and the arts. An essentialism of the dark side, as it were. George Steiner put it most forcefully when he asked how the Nazi genocide could have been perpetrated by lovers of Beethoven and Mozart. So did John Carey when he asked recently, *What Good are the Arts?*[43] The danger of essentialist arguments is that the gun can be turned on you.

I would prefer a pragmatic approach, involving a defence of the innovations, the fresh knowledge, and the new friends for culture, that come from close attention to what are usually called the 'ancillary' benefits of culture and creativity, such as economic opportunity and innovation, social inclusion, and educational advantage. It's best to keep moving forward on several fronts, lest one be outflanked or forced into retreat.

This essay, then, has stressed the opportunity to significantly broaden the support base, from culture and the arts to the creative community (or class). Richard Florida is very aware, as I am myself, of the problems associated with galvanising a consciousness among such a diverse group[44] and nevertheless, while it is a group that may have little of the solidarity evidenced by artists, it is the object of much state attention. This gives us the opportunity to 'mainstream the claims', to emphasise a small-business and demand-driven ethos as a strong complement to the charismatic, supply-side ethos of the national artistic leadership. This places emphasis on career development and opportunities through occupation as much as industry sector—combining the arts with market-driven, commercial ventures and employment and emphasising sustainability and impact as functions of an economy-wide vision.

The 'price' to be paid is that the special status attributed to the arts and culture is folded into the need for creativity across the economy and society. To reach our destination, we must take the long way round.

Endnotes

1   *Creative Industries: Contracts between Art and Commerce* (Cambridge, Mass.: Harvard University Press, 2000).

2   *Capturing Cultural Value: How Culture Has Become a Tool of Government Policy* (London: Demos, 2004), available at www.demos.co.uk/catalogue/culturalvalue (accessed 10 April 2006).

3   For an excellent short overview, see Terry Flew, *New Media: An Introduction* (Oxford: OUP, 2002), Chap. 6. A more detailed introduction is provided by *Creative Industries*, ed. by John Hartley (Malden, MA: Blackwell Publishing, 2005).

4   It is probable, however, that the term was originally used in Australia in 1994 by Terry Cutler and Roger Buckeridge, *Commerce in Content: Building Australia's International future in Interactive Multimedia Markets*, a report for the Dept of Industry, Science and Technology, CSIRO and the Broadband Services Expert Group, Dept of Industry, Science and Technology, Canberra, available at www.nla.gov.au/misc/cutler/cutlercp (accessed 10 April 2006).

5   See www.culture.gov.uk (accessed 10 April 2006).

6   For a fuller account, see Stuart Cunningham, 'The Humanities, Creative Arts and International Innovation Agendas', in *Innovation and Tradition: The Arts, Humanities and the Knowledge Economy*, ed. by Jane Kenway, Elizabeth Bullen and Simon Robb (New York: Peter Lang, 2004), pp. 113-24.

7   See www.mcg.go.kr/english/section/vision (accessed 10 April 2006), and *The Third Master Plan for Informatization, 2002-2006* (Ministry of Information and Communication, Korea: 2006).

8   See Doobo Shim, 'Hybridity and the Korean wave', *Media, Culture and Society*, 28.1 (2006), 25-54.

9   For a summary of Taiwan's creative industry policy, see *Challenge 2008: The Six-Year National Development Plan*, available at www.gio.gov.tw/taiwan-website/4-oa/20020521/2002052101 (accessed 10 April 2006). See also Tsai Wen-ting, 'Cultural and creative industries: wedding commerce with culture', *Sinorama*, no. 4 (2004), 6.

10 *Baseline Study on Hong Kong's Creative Industries*, 2003, Centre for Cultural Policy Research, University of King Kong and Hong Kong Trade Development Council, 2002, *Creative Industries in Hong Kong*, available at www.tdctrade.com/econforum/tdc/tdc020902 (accessed 10 April 2006).

11 For an overview of Singapore's policies and links to a number of key policy documents, see www.mica.gov.sg/mica_business/b_creative (accessed 10 April 2006).

12 For an overview of New Zealand's policies, see 'Developing Creative Industries in New Zealand', available at both www.nzte.govt.nz/section/11756.aspx#overview and www.ntze.govt.nz/common/files/ses-creative05.pdf (accessed 10 April 2006).

13 See, for example, Nicholas Garnham, 'From Cultural to Creative Industries: An analysis of the implications of the "creative industries" approach to arts and media policy making in the United Kingdom', *International Journal of Cultural Policy*, 11 (2005), 15-29.

14 See www.gov.cn/english/2005-11/26/content_109854 (accessed 10 April 2006).

15 See J. O'Connor, 'A New Modernity? The Arrival

of "Creative Industries" in China' and D. Hui, and 'From Cultural to Creative Industries—Strategies for Chaoyang District, Beijing', *International Journal of Cultural Studies*, 9.3 (2006).

16 See www.cep.culture.gov.uk (accessed 10 April 2006).

17 See UK Creative Industries Minister James Purnell, 4 November 2005, available at www.culture.gov.uk/global/press_notices/archive_2005/147_05 (accessed 10 April 2006).

18 See www.sdi.qld.gov.au/dsdweb/v3/guis/templates/content/gui_cue_cntnhtml.cfm?id=2223 (accessed 10 April 2006).

19 See Coopers & Lybrand, Multimedia Industry Group report, *Excellence in Content: The Focus for Australian Investment in Multimedia Content* (Sydney, June 1995); *Networking Australia's Future: The Final Report of the Broadband Services Expert Group* (Canberra: Australian Govt. Pub. Service, 1995); *Creative Nation: Commonwealth Cultural Policy* (Dept. of Communications, Information and the Arts: Canberra, 1994).

20 For a detailed account of this history, see Tom O'Regan and Mark David Ryan, 'From Multimedia to Digital Content and Applications: Remaking Policy for the Digital Content Industries', *Media International Australia incorporating Culture & Policy*, No. 112 (2005), 28-49.

21 *Creative Industries Cluster Study* (Dept of Communications, Information Technology and the Arts (DCITA): Canberra, 2004) available at www.cultureandrecreation.gov.au/cics; *Digital Content Industry Action Agenda*, available at: www.dcita.gov.au/arts/film_digital/digital_content_industry_action_agenda; Prime Minister's Science, Engineering and Innovation

Council (PMSEIC) Working Group, 2005, *The Role of Creativity in the Innovation Economy*, available at: www.dest.gov.au/NR/rdonlyres/B1EF82EF-08D5-427E-B7E4-69D41C61D495/8625/finalPMSEICReport_WEBversion.pdf (accessed 10 April 2006).

22 *Creativity is Big Business: A Framework for the Future* (Dept of State Development, Trade and Innovation), available at: www.sdi.qld.gov.au/dsdweb/v3/document/objdirctrled/nonsecure/pdf/2698.pdf (accessed 10 April 2006).

23 See www.ozco.gov.au/news_and_hot_topics/news/creative_innovation/files/3375/CIS%20public%20FINAL.pdf (accessed 8 May 2006).

24 See also Stuart Cunningham, 'Match Seller or Sparkplug? The Human Sciences and Business', *B-HERT (Business-Higher Education Round Table) News*, issue 22 (July 2005), 8-10.

25 *The Creative Economy: How People Make Money from Ideas* (Harmondsworth: Penguin, 2001), p. 85.

26 *The Rise of the Creative Class: And How It's Transforming Work, Leisure, Community and Everyday Life* (New York: Basic Books, 2002).

27 See Terry Cutler's foreword to the Australian edition of Florida's *Rise of the Creative Class* (North Melbourne: Pluto Press, 2002), pp. vii-xi.

28 See 'How big are the Creative Industries in Australia? The interim findings' and 'Taking the ruler to the Creative Industries: How, why and to what effect', at wiki.cci.edu.au/confluence. See also P. Higgs and others, *The Ecology of Queensland Design* (CIRAC, QUT, 2005), available at eprint.qut.edu.au/archive/00002410 (accessed 10 April 2006) and CIRAC and SGS Economics and Planning, *Mapping Queensland's Creative Industries: Economic Fundamentals* (CIRAC, QUT, 2005), available at:

eprint.qut.edu.au/archive/00002425 (accessed 10 April 2006).

29 See cultureandrecreation.gov.au/cics (accessed 10 April 2006).

30 See the survey in Margaret Bruce and Lucy Daly, *International Evidence on Design: Near Final Report for the DTI* (Manchester Business School, University of Manchester, 2005).

31 *Economics and Culture* (Cambridge: CUP, 2001), p. 112.

32 *Does Australia Need a Cultural Policy?* Platform Paper No. 7 (Sydney: Currency House, 2006), p. 39.

34 The ABC secured an additional $88 million over three years in the 2006 budget for Australian and digital content production. This will contribute to its ability to innovate.

35 'The End of Serious Journalism?', in *Barons to Bloggers: Confronting Media Power*, ed. by Jonathan Mills, The Alfred Deakin Debate, vol.1 (Melbourne: Miegunyah Press, 2005), p. 67.

36 See www.carenegie.org/reporter/10/news/index.html (accessed 10 April 2006).

37 *Creative Industries*, pp. 2ff.

38 London & New York: Routledge, 2004.

39 J. Stanley Metcalfe, *Evolutionary Economics and Creative Destruction* (London & New York: Routledge, 1998); B.J. Loasby, *Knowledge, Institutions and Evolution in Economics* (London & New York: Routledge, 1999); Jason Potts, *The New Evolutionary Microeconomics: Complexity, Competence and Adaptive Behaviour* (London: Edward Elgar Publishing, 2000).

40 See *Innovation Systems in the Service Economy: Measurement and Case Study Analysis*, ed. by J. Stanley Metcalfe and Ian Miles (Boston: Kluwer

Academic, 2000); *Services and the Knowledge-Based Economy*, ed. by Mark Boden and Ian Miles (London & New York: Continuum, 2000).

41 See www.mmu.ac.uk/h-ss/mipc/foci/mission (accessed 10 April 2006).

42 CIRAC, QUT and Cutler & Co., *Research and Innovation Systems in the Production of Digital Content*, Report for the National Office for the Information Economy (September 2003), available at: www.cultureandrecreation.gov.au/cics/Research_and_ innovation_systems_in_production_of_digital_content.pdf (accessed 10 April 2006) and CIRAC, QUT and Cutler & Co., *Research and Innovation Systems in the Production of Digital Content and Applications*, Creative Industries Cluster Study, Vol. 3 (DCITA, Canberra, 2004), pp. 9-67. A summary version was published as Stuart Cunningham and others, 'From "Culture" to "Knowledge": An Innovation Systems Approach to the Content Industries', in *Accounting for Culture: Thinking through Cultural Citizenship*, ed. by Caroline Andrew and others (Ottawa: University of Ottawa Press, 2005), pp. 104-23.

43 See *Capturing Cultural Value: How Culture has become a Tool of Government Policy* (London: Demos, 2005), and *Cultural Value and the Crisis of Legitimacy: Why Culture needs a Democratic Mandate* (London: Demos, 2006), available at www.demos.co.uk/catalogue/culturallegitimacy (accessed 10 April 2006).

44 *Language and Silence: Essays 1958-1966* (Harmondsworth: Penguin Books, 1969); John Carey, *What Good are the Arts?* (London: Faber & Faber, 2005).

45 *Rise of the Creative Class*, Chap. 17.

Readers' Forum

Publication of Amanda Card's Platform Paper, *Body for Hire: the State of Dance in Australia*, was an opportunity for a 'call to action' to raise the profile of dance in Australia.

Jennifer McLachlan is Director of Dance, Australia Council for the Arts.

Reading Amanda's often very personal observations made me reflect on my own background in dance. Having trained in Cecchetti and RAD at the Scottish Ballet, and later in Graham and Cunningham techniques at London Contemporary Dance School, I realised that my dance lineage would leave me horribly unemployable as a 'body for hire'. Happily for me, getting a job in the contemporary dance sector isn't nearly that simple.

Many leading choreographers want and need to work with a particular dancer or group of dancers to develop their work, their vocabulary and their form. I don't—for a second—believe they do so because 'funding structures dictate it'. I also believe that contemporary dance already has a strong history of repertory-based companies employing 'bodies for hire'. I believe that this encapsulates a weakness in Amanda's paper. In trying to force the diversity of the Australian dance scene into a narrow schema, in many ways she misses the point.

Perhaps we *could* engineer a series of state-based contemporary dance supergroups. This might produce a strong sector in which dancers have a lucrative career path, but it would undoubtedly have major repercussions across the rest of the field. Either way, it is not the role of any funding body to dictate the development of the artform in this way—unless there is universal support across the sector. I'm yet to hear this groundswell of opinion.

And while the dance sector *should* get more money from governments, the reality of budget processes is nowhere near that simple. There is no question that improved support for the sector remains one of the Australia Council for the Arts' fundamental aims. The long-standing (and continuing) lobbying efforts of the Australia Council and the dance sector in making the case for increased funding testifies to the difficulties involved in the budget process.

While getting a boost in the direct funding of the dance sector is a difficult process, there are a number of other indirect ways that the Australia Council's Dance Board is channelling more dollars into dance.

Working with other parts of the Australia Council—Major Performing Arts Board, Key Organisations, Community Partnerships and Market Development, Aboriginal and Torres Strait Islander Arts Board and our new Inter-Arts Office—has already borne substantial dividends for the sector.

Different parts of the Australia Council are working together through programs such as the touring initiative Mobile States (with the Theatre Board, Inter-Arts Office and performing arts venues across the country) and Indigenous dance infrastructure development (with the ATSIA Board and state and territory ministries). We are also working more broadly with the Australian Government on programs and initiatives such as Playing Australia, New Australian Stories, Major Festivals Initiative and Young and Emerging Artist initiatives such as SPARK and Take Your Partner.

There are also a number of strategies and activities in capacity-building across the sector. These include our recent announcement of SCOPE—an exciting program to assist dancers to increase their earned income, being run with Ausdance and the Australian Institute of Sport. This project is one of the Australia Council's major restructure.

In all, the Australia Council supports the Australian dance sector to the tune of around $11 million—with more than $3.4 million of this money being distributed through the Dance Board to what Amanda considers the 'lower end of town'.

It's companies from this 'lower end of town' that are selling-out venues in Paris; are in high demand across Europe; and were recently the 'talk of the town' in New York. So much is already being achieved on such limited resources.

However, we are unlikely to get contemporary dance out of our (self-perceived) ghetto simply by asking for more government money. In the UK, the influx of funds to the arts coming from the government's lottery system undoubtedly gave the dance sector a boost. More than this, however, it was a concerted effort to connect with new audiences and build partnerships in the community that took dance to its current flag-bearing status in the performing arts.

I agree wholeheartedly with Amanda on one point, one that I have heard repeatedly across the country—that now is the time when we can all make a difference.

We urgently need to come together as a sector, including state and federal funding bodies, to find new ways to back the creativity and innovation that are the hallmark of Australian contemporary dance.

We need to find new and exciting ways to get more people interested in dance; to have more creative dance staged; and to encourage more people to come and enjoy it. And we can only do these things by working together.

David Spurgeon is a senior lecturer, and co-ordinator of the Dance Program, in the School of Media, Film and Theatre at The University of New South Wales.

I congratulate Amanda Card on her provocative and insightful look at aspects of dance in Australia, and would like to comment on just two of the issues she raises.

During a three-month study leave last year, which I spent at the new Centre national de danse in Paris, I had the opportunity to watch a number of video recordings of dance performances recently given at the Centre. I was disturbed to see how many 'dance' items held in, and subsidised by, the Centre featured performers who appeared to have had very little dance training or experience. I agree with Amanda's assertion that here in Australia we have a strong group of 'bodies for hire', dancers with finely honed dance technique, further inscribed by the acquisition of other movement disciplines. Indeed, we have dancers who, to quote Amanda's analogy, can 'run like a runner'. My point is that I feel that the dance scene in Australia has many instances of exciting practice because we have dancers, not non-dancers, experimenting with new movement and new performance forms. Australia's 'bodies for hire' can invest the most mundane movement with a kinaesthetic—an 'imprinting', 'multi-layering', perhaps—significance. This was entirely missing from the many obscure and self-referential, non-dance performance pieces that I watched in Paris, pieces which, nevertheless, were advertised, and received funding, as 'dance'.

Secondly, with regard to Amanda's discussion of the 'role of institutions in the redefinition of independence', I believe that many tertiary institutions can and, indeed, do play a supportive role in the nurturing of new choreographic talent. They do more than simply produce graduates for the job market; they can, for example, offer freelance choreographers living on the smell of an oily rag the occasional chance to practise their craft at no cost. At the University of New South Wales, where I co-ordinate the Dance Program, I have two dance studios at my disposal and ninety full-time students, all intent on teaching dance in high schools and all anxious for any opportunity to dance. I find myself, therefore, in a position, to provide such a choreographer with not only space and time, but also, given ample time to make the necessary arrangements, several dozen dance-students' bodies. And all this at no cost to either the University or the choreographer. In return, I can expect some teaching or choreography—sometimes for a reduced fee and sometimes, depending on circumstances, for the usual professional fee. I also benefit by having on campus an expert dance-maker, who is prepared to help out with advising and assessing the students' dance work. I am sure that this kind of loosely symbiotic relationship, or something similar, has been experimented with elsewhere in other institutions. It deserves to be more widespread. For the last few years I have been fortunate enough to be able to call upon the services and talents of Sue Healey in this capacity: she teaches, on a casual basis, in the undergraduate program, and, when her busy schedule permits, choreographs for us. In return, we can make available to her the keys to the studios, where, subject to availability and mutual convenience, she is free to rehearse her own dance group. Sue is, as it were, a 'part of the family'. It is a 'win-win' arrangement for both parties.